Leading From the Heart

Melissa Bird

Leading From the Heart

Published by:

Thought Leader Press

Hardcover ISBN: 978-1-61343-186-3

Paperback ISBN: 978-1-61343-187-0

Ebook ISBN: 978-1-61343-188-7

I dedicate this work to my dad, whom I read to every morning while he got ready for work. And to my mom, who taught me that reading is the most important activity one can engage in. Thanks for always letting me fall asleep with a book in my hands.

Table of Contents

ACKNOWLEDGEMENTS

I would like to thank my wonderful husband, without whom I would not have found my way in this world. In the midst of heartbreak in 2010, I prayed for someone who would love me for who I am, and my prayers were answered by this beautiful man.

To my children, it is always an honor to be your mom. Thank you for choosing me time and again to love you, to guide you, and to support you in your beautiful lives.

To my lifelong friend Kristen, I will always remember, even if you forget.

To Margaret, who filled our play time with books.

And to all of you reading this book, thank you for believing there is a different way for us to lead.

LEADING FROM THE HEART

I am Dr. Melissa Bird. I am a descendant of the Shivwits Band of Paiutes and the daughter of Christina and Vern. My story starts when my father committed suicide when I was six. That was in 1980, when society was not talking about suicide and mental health. We certainly were not talking about Native American people the way we do today. My father was a mixed-race man who suffered from depression. He could not talk about these things because his identity was shameful and disgraceful in conservative Utah at that time.

This is a critical part of my story, because I was not allowed to talk about my father and how he died. My mother was so devastated by his death that she didn't want to talk about him, so I was not allowed to do so. This meant that I was not allowed to ask questions about who I was as his daughter.

I think the beauty of turning 50 this year and being able to look back and reflect on my life is realizing how difficult things must have been for my father. I know how my father died, and as I age I am realizing how difficult it must have been for him to live as a Native American and a white man surrounded by Mormon culture in the state of Utah.

His death has affected my entire life. How could it not? It was such a huge loss for my mom, my sister, and me.

“

I exhale a promise to myself
to always speak what is
in my heart.

As a social worker and a leader in my own community, I have helped people process grief. This role came about as a result of my father's death. My expertise in grief is born from a lifetime of processing his death and the death of many others. Here in the United States, we don't grieve well. I believe that one of the most beautiful things to come out of the COVID-19 pandemic is that we were forced into a global grief cycle. The last time we did that was the Second World War. The pandemic brought to the surface many of the feelings, emotions, and thoughts that we had bottled up so tightly inside us.

This caused me to realize that my role as a grief facilitator was shifting and changing. I needed to connect with more people in power, people who had the opportunity to shift policy and deeply impact our broader communities. The people that we work with on a daily basis aren't just coming to a job. They are coming to a job carrying a set of complex emotions and likely, grief.

“

This human experience is wholly unpredictable and gloriously wild.

I used to be the lobbyist for Planned Parenthood of Utah. I got paid to cause good trouble alongside some remarkable policy makers and advocates at the state and national level. As a bisexual, feminist woman who grew up in Utah, I have been in situations where I engaged in community change that could have been seen as controversial. But because I was anchored in knowing that the work I was doing wasn't just for me, but for the entire state of Utah, when I was put in those positions where I was supposed to keep my mouth shut, I did the opposite. That is heart-centered, soulful leadership.

What we are craving is connection... What we are missing is the collective. We throw around these buzzwords, such as colonization, white supremacy, patriarchy, and feminism, but we are not getting into the substantive bits of what that truly means for the collective.

'Complicated grief' is the term for unresolved or unacknowledged grief, but I think all grief is complicated. I don't know why we have that term. Why is some grief special and complicated, and some grief is just grief? If an 85-year-old grandma dies, is that supposed to be considered 'normal' grief?

All grief is complicated, and we are all grieving the loss of something. We are grieving the loss of a life we were promised, especially those of us who were '80s kids. We were running around outside until the lights came on. Everything was sort of okay. We could grow up and buy a house, we could buy a car, and we could go to college without getting into too much debt. It wasn't excruciating. Now, we are grieving the life that we thought we were going to get. We are grieving the promise of the 'American Dream', whatever that means.

In addition, we are grieving a planet that appears to be in crisis. While we have accelerated global warming through what we like to call 'technological innovation' and taking more resources than we could possibly ever need, it is incumbent on us to recognize that Mother Earth is tired of the way we are treating her.

“

The complexities of life are what creates its beauty. Lack of connection to Earth is what creates confusion in our souls.

I said to someone last year, "The Earth is a middle-aged woman. She's pissed off, and she's hot and tired. She doesn't want to be treated like crap anymore, and she's showing us that. We just don't like what she's showing us because we don't have any control over the hurricanes, the fires, the volcanoes, the earthquakes, or the typhoons. She's colder than cold one minute, and she's hotter than hot the next."

The Earth has been doing this for millenia. She has constantly adapted, evolved, and changed to take care of all the beings on the planet. She is not going anywhere, but we are.

“

When we allow the divine to hold us, when we have true faith and surrender, there is literally nothing that requires control.

This is another form of grief: we don't have control over this planet, even though patriarchal, white supremacist structures have told us we do. We have to surrender to the idea that we have absolutely no control. Yes, we have choices, and that is the journey of life. We are not here to control other people. We are not here to control outcomes. We are here to contribute, to connect, and to look at the world around us and take the hint that there might be a better way. The way of releasing.

For many of us, we are walking around holding heavy backpacks full of perfectionism, worry, and the weariness of everyday life. The way of releasing invites us into a different practice where each one of us stops holding on to the weight of a life we thought we would have, so we can embrace the freedom of the life we do have.

This idea can oftentimes make people double down and hold on tighter. I invite you to loosen your grip, talk to the people around you, and ask, "How are you doing? What's going on in your life? What do you need?" I learned all of that from the death of my father.

In the recent work that I have been doing since COVID, I have learned that people want to listen to their internal voices. They want to understand their intuition.

Intuition has become such a buzzword. It's become sexy to talk about, which I find to be so bizarre. We all have an intuition, and we all have a soul. We are here in these bodies to give our souls an experience.

“

When you enjoy yourself
and pay attention to life,
even the smallest details,
you spark your magic
and your intuition grows.
This expansion is what we
are craving.

”

There is a lot of writing on this topic. We are trained not to listen to our intuition. Whether it's developing seven healthy habits or finding five things to become the kind of leader you want to be, we are always trying to distill the process into clearly defined steps.

People want a sales funnel that says, "Here you go! You're on your way to becoming an intuitive leader." However, the way intuition speaks is different for everyone. The way my intuition talks to me is not the way somebody else's intuition talks to them.

You can't distill intuitive leadership into a seven-step process. It requires us to be willing and vulnerable. We have to listen to our hearts, risk loss, and risk someone seeing who we actually are on the inside.

Being a vulnerable leader requires that we humble ourselves and recognize our shortcomings. That takes grace.

In the process I teach ('The Art of the Graceful Revolution'), I talk about the idea that revolution is not always found in protests, yelling, or anger. Sometimes, protest comes from looking inside yourself and saying, "What do I see for myself, my community, and the neighborhood around me? What do I want for us? What is in our collective best interest?"

“

I believe that radical, graceful revolution can take place when we lead with cords of human kindness, if we handfast ourselves with bands of love.

Intuitive leadership requires that you ask the question, "What is the best and highest good for all?"

That answer is different for all of us. It leads to some great starting points to figure out how to begin changing culture and dialogue, whether it's where you work, where you live, or who you interact with. All of a sudden, it's about more than, "What's in it for me?"

That is the only question a lot of people are asking right now. It's not just occurring in the United States' political sphere, but also in global politics. I almost envision it as people in power pushing their thumbs down on other people. How much more punitive can we get? How much more can we shove people down to control them?

If we can regulate people's bodies, people's speech, or war, then many people will feel better and more in control as leaders.

Corporations are doing the same thing. What would happen if we stopped trying to push our thumbs down on everyone? What if we opened our hands and said, "I don't have all the answers. Could you help me? I don't know everything."

That entirely undermines the idea of creating seven habits and of people saying, "Here are five things you can do to be a truly intuitive leader."

There is no magic pill, and yet, everybody wants one.

What separates me from other leaders is that I talk about soulful leadership. I discuss the need to connect to our spirits and to believe in something that is bigger than us.

Some call it God, some call it the universe, and some call it spirit or source. There are a million words for it, but what's important is to listen to that small voice inside of us that says, "No, there's a better way and this is it." We must permit ourselves to surrender to that and to not worry about what other people are going to say. Instead, we must truly lead from the heart.

“

Remember to listen to that inner guide inside you. There is a little voice in there. Sometimes it is quietly whispering, sometimes it is pounding down the door, but it is always there telling you exactly what you need to hear. Listen to the whispers of your heart. They are your guiding light.

”

When we lead from the voices of our hearts, we don't harm other people, animals, or the planet. We start to surrender to the idea that we don't have all the answers. We give ourselves over to the notion that we need a community around us, like our fellow employees, our staff, or our team, to help inform our decisions.

What do you know? How do you envision the future of the world?

When we ask, "I don't know it all. Can you help me?" we are connecting back to the collective. People resist intuitive leadership because it requires admitting, "I don't know everything. I don't have all the answers. In fact, I need to bring in people who can help inform me." That is why people run away screaming from it.

People talk about the mind, body, and spirit. You hear this in the self-help world all the time. Somehow, we have equated spirituality with religion and religion with spirituality. Those two things are entirely separate, but both are woven into the fabric of who we are as human beings.

Even if you don't consider yourself religious or spiritual, you can't deny that there is a soul in your body that is here to have an experience. That's the truth.

This is part of the Graceful Revolution. We have to admit that there are things we don't have the answers to because the answers are so vast that we can't possibly comprehend them.

"

Think of your life as a giant mosaic puzzle. What pieces fit and what pieces don't? Where have you had to change the strategy to reach the grand vision of a finished product?

"

This concept disrupts and dismantles the idea that you become a leader because you are knowledgeable. People may say, "You have all the answers, so you can be a leader." That is the way that people in control often think. A lot of people have experience that has nothing to do with the way we define traditional leadership.

For years, I have wrestled with the fact that I am considered a leader. I grapple with soulful leadership and leading from the heart, which together have brought me gifts, wisdom, and connections.

Listening to your intuition and engaging in soulful leadership is beautiful. You get a lot more out of it because you are not trying to prescribe the conversation. You are allowing it to evolve and open on its own, and then you look at what is there. To simply be quiet while someone else is talking is a very ancient way of thinking.

Being open to ideas that don't necessarily resonate with you is very difficult for people. When we are open to other ideas, there will be little moments where you go, "Oh, I can see how that might be a good idea."

The world has become so polarized. We get into this all-or-nothing and either/or type of thinking. Socially, leading from our intuition puts us in the space of both/and. When I teach this in my workshops or the speeches I give, people become much more open to living in the both/and. They become curious about the world around them and how they can lead from their heart.

*To **lead** in revolution.*

*To **hold** in compassion.*

*To **love** without reason.*

*To **be** without doing.*

*To **act** with the planet.*

*To **share** in communion.*

*To **laugh** with abandon.*

*To **praise** with exaltation.*

*To **love**, to **love**, to **love**.*

We can be both angry and happy. When we are acting from the space of both/and, we can learn from it. We can both know the answer and be willing to hear other answers. When we get ourselves out of that either/or binary thinking, we open up whatever space we are leading from to infinite possibilities. That can be intimidating because we often can't see the infinite possibilities from the start.

This is our natural way of being. We are 'humans being', not human beings. Since we are 'humans being', we intuitively recognize that we are intricately tied to the planet. We are not separate or above it, nor are we in charge of or in control of it.

We do not need to save the planet. She is fine all by herself, and she can save herself. We have to listen to the planet, just like we have to listen to our colleagues, friends, and families.

If we allow ourselves to think about how we are all 'humans being', how we are all here learning different lessons, having different experiences, engaging with the world, and learning how to love, grieve, and engage with each other, then it's not so scary to look up at the sky and think, 'I'm part of the vastness of the universe.' The billions of us who are on the planet right now are all here at the same time. We can wonder why that is instead of having to control why that is.

The answer is a conversation that not everybody is going to love or be open to.

WE CRAVE CONNECTION

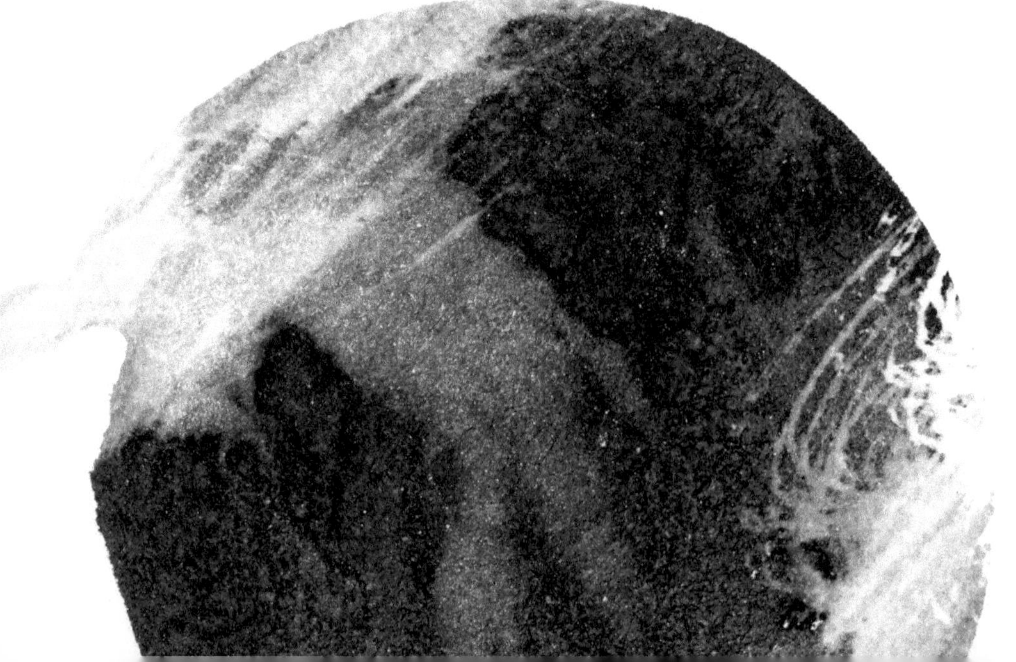

“

There is wisdom in connecting in a world that is convinced that it thrives in disconnection.

Being open to discomfort and keeping your eyes open means acknowledging that there is not just one way to do things. People often think, 'I'm going to help facilitate this conversation, get all my ideas out, and then everybody's going to love me. It's going to be awesome.' That's not how we get in touch with what we can do to change our communities or make an impact.

Perhaps our communities don't need to be changed. Perhaps we just need to hear each other out without doing anything else.

I was thinking about this while recovering from a recent surgery. Why do we believe we have to act? Why can't we just listen to each other without having to do anything? What if we could just have the coffee klatch or the stitch n' bitch and just listen to each other without having to fix anything?

I was telling my daughter the other day about Scottish plaid, kilts, and my ancestry. I said, "The women used to sit in these big circles with wool and work it back and forth, and while they worked they would talk and sing."

I imagine those women just sitting there talking back and forth. They didn't have to fix anything or 'do' anything. They didn't have to wrangle their kids. Their families were fine. They just worked the wool.

When my mother used to go to her stitch n' bitch, the women would sit around sewing, knitting, and just talking. None of them had to fix one another, and none of them had to have a solution for their best friend's problem.

A lot of people come to me for advice. I have gotten into the practice of asking my friends, "Do you need me to give you advice, or do you just need someone to hear you?" Nine times out of ten we just need someone to listen to us.

If you are a leader, such as a boss, a thought leader, or an elected official, I invite you to think about the idea that perhaps people just need to open up to you. Perhaps they just need to feel like they have had their voices heard. They don't need you to have an answer, and they don't need you to do anything.

“

Expanding into spirituality
gives us the opportunity
to engage with faith
in something greater
than we are.

Allowing yourself to be an intuitive, heart-led listener can be a relief. You can listen to what people are saying without having to come up with a solution to their problem.

I don't want to have all the answers, but I do want to hear and connect with people. That is a completely different way of approaching leadership.

Soulful leadership is not just about community, and it's not just about the collective. We can talk about those concepts, but what we are truly craving is connection. We desire to be seen and heard without someone thinking that we are wrong.

When it comes to our own experiences, we make assumptions that what is in the best interest of others is in our best interest, too.

Most specializations and industries, even social work, are built on research that decides what is in the community's best interest. But most social welfare research, for example, is based on assumptions that people of color, women, homeless people, and people with disabilities are somehow at a disadvantage.

Even grant-making structures are like this. We assume that someone is at a disadvantage, so we decide to be benevolent and give them money. We assume that what they need is the same thing that those of us who are making these decisions, the people in power, need. We assume people need a home, food, and medical care. We make assumptions about what makes a person happy.

People in power, people with money, and people doing the research are all asking the wrong questions. They are making assumptions rather than asking, "What do you need?"

Everybody needs something different. We have to be open to the differences in people's experiences.

“

*Through joy we will inspire.
Through listening we will
be comforted.*

We organize people into boxes to make a difference in our communities. Everybody talks about getting a college education and how important it is to get a degree. New research just came out that nine out of ten Gen Zers say, "Screw getting an education! I'll just go into the trades and move on with my life. I'm not going to college."[1] To that I say, "Yay!"

There is a disconnect between what people need to feel empowered and what others think they need.

Giving people the space to express their own experiences allows us to gracefully navigate the unknown. We are afraid of the mass chaos that might occur if everybody got their own say, but

---

1 *"Walton Family Foundation - Gallup Voices of Gen Z Study: Year 2 Annual Survey Report." Gallup, 2024. https://nextgeninsights.waltonfamilyfoundation.org/wp-content/uploads/2024/08/Walton_Gallup_Voices-of-Gen-Z_Year-2-2024-Final-Report.pdf*

in reality it would lead to us being able to better navigate the unknown by recognizing our communal experiences. We can hold space for that when we find little threads woven through our experiences.

YOU DON'T HAVE TO HAVE ALL THE ANSWERS

“

Being tender with ourselves allows us to see this life through beautiful awe-filled reverence.

We have been trained to think that if we are going to be an expert in a field, we have to know everything about it. If we are going to make an impact on our lives and our communities, we have to know everything. If someone says, "Well, what about this? Have you thought about it this way?" we think we have to be able to say, "Yes, absolutely, I have thought about it that way."

When we think we have to have all of the answers, it forces us into an all-or-nothing mindset.

When we allow ourselves to be human, we realize that we only have answers based on our own lived experiences. We don't have answers that reflect a communal experience.

We don't know everything. In fact, we can't know everything. It is society that teaches us to believe that good leaders have all the answers. We look to leaders and think, 'Well, they know the answer to the problem! I don't have to worry about figuring it out myself.'

If we permit ourselves to recognize that we don't need another degree, more training, another course, or another level of education, we can say, "I don't know the answer, and I'm willing to connect with the person who does," or "I'm willing to find the person who can help me." Be willing to put yourself out there and say, "Hey, I need help."

Asking for help is one of the most difficult things a leader can do. It is certainly a challenge for most human beings in general. People don't like to ask for help. We like to think that we can solve all our problems on our own, but we can't.

We are not meant to figure things out on our own. We are meant to help one another.

“

Put your energy into how it could be.

If you look back over eons of time, you can see the way communities used to be structured. Before the Industrial Revolution, a person's last name would be based on their trade. People were ironworkers, healers, and bakers, and they were named accordingly. That has shifted over time, because somehow we have bought into the lie that we must become everything to everybody.

The bottom line is that we can't do everything. We have to ask for help.

When we feel helpless, we often ask, "What can I do?" It's almost like a prayer. The answer often is, "You can't do anything."

Oftentimes, there is nothing to be done. When someone close to you dies, the first thing people ask you is, "What can I do? What can I do to ease your pain? Can I cook for you?" Where I grew up in Utah, everyone brings a casserole to the grieving family. People bringing others food when someone dies is a universal practice.

Instead of allowing space for grief, people keep themselves busy to avoid feelings of sadness, anguish, and anger.

“

The way to have more faith is to allow more, surrender more, and trust more.

People get into the cycle of doing, doing, doing to avoid their grief.

We do the same thing when we are trying to perpetuate feelings of joy or happiness. We ask ourselves, "What can I do to keep this feeling going? I'm going to keep doing, doing, doing, more, more, and more."

We are not supposed to do so much. That's why people say, "I don't have enough time. I'm too stressed out."

The practice of reflection becomes more important when we are leading from the heart. When we believe there is something we can do to make ourselves feel better, make something right, or to hold on to a feeling, we put ourselves out of alignment with the natural course of being. We push ourselves out of the flow and don't allow answers to naturally appear before us.

Leading from a space of quiet resolve connects us to the mystery of life. We begin to be curious about what is going to happen next. However, we are taught that we are supposed to be in action mode constantly. We focus on the action of doing when truly we could cut out half the work we do.

A lot of us wake up with a to-do list in our minds. Immediately, we start thinking about what we have to do that day. A practice that I have begun to engage in is to wake up and think, 'I wonder what's going to happen today.'

This creates space for the mystery of life and disrupts the habit of 'doing' just as we are coming back into our bodies and waking up. Before you've even moved your legs over the side of the bed, what if you just laid there for five seconds and thought, 'I wonder what's going to happen today?'

This practice completely opens up the day for possibility. You still have the to-do list, but the to-do list becomes something different when you wonder how it's going to play out.

If you engage with life from a space of wonder and curiosity, you don't have to do quite so much.

"

May you find the beauty and moments of peace every day. May you stand bravely in the truth of your own story. May you be patient with yourself and others as we wake each day to new adventures.

"

One of the things we learned from the pandemic is that people don't want to operate the way they were operating before. They don't want to work the way they used to work, and they don't want to talk the way they used to talk.

People want to feel like they can make a difference in the place where they spend most of their time, which is at work. They want to feel engaged in making a difference in their lives and their communities. They don't want to be spoken 'at' anymore. They want to be a part of the process.

When we, as leaders, allow ourselves to think in a different way, we begin to learn what's going to help our companies and governments run better. We need to think from the space of asking, wondering, and engaging, not from the space of doing.

The reality is that we still need leaders. There has always been a medicine man, a chief, or a shaman. There has always been someone people would go to for information and guidance. That person would listen and take in what the community had to say.

I dream that people in power will start thinking about how we can connect in a more communal way. I recently talked to some people about the movement to work from home and how it changed downtown economies. Bakeries, coffee shops, and lunch counters are closing because there is no one downtown anymore to support them.

We all think, 'Working from home is a great idea. Now I don't have to pay rent on my

32,000-square-foot office.' We don't think about what that means for Larry the hot dog guy down the street.

Somehow, we have to shift our thinking away from what is best for the company, the office, and maintaining the status quo and start thinking about what is best for the people around us.

“

Tension with our fellow humans can't live in grace. Grace is fluid. Respond in grace.

THE CONVERSATION

It's hard to be vulnerable with the truth about your experience to people in power. You risk being judged for your experience, people not believing your experience is valid, or being completely dismissed.

Not everybody loves having difficult conversations. Telling our truth requires taking a chance. This can be uncomfortable for people, and it makes others uncomfortable to hear you speak about your experience.

Once we admit that we are all a little bit uncomfortable with telling our stories, speaking our truths, and trying to create change allows us to be open to hearing what other people have to say.

There is a phrase about speaking truth to power. The people in power don't want to hear the truth, and you are not going to love going through the process of trying to get people to hear you just to be dismissed again.

People are not going to behave the way we want them to. They're just not. Our friends don't behave the way we want them to, and neither do our kids. Even our own partners don't do that.

If we give ourselves permission to not have expectations going into truth-telling conversations, we become willing to take the risk to try, and then something will shift.

Just because we don't get the outcome we hope for doesn't mean we are not getting the outcome that's in the best interest of the highest good.

“

It all falls into place at exactly the right time. You haven't failed, you haven't lost. You are on a journey and each moment leads to the next.

I often say that it took us a long time to get here as a country. It's going to take us even longer to fix, change, or dismantle all of the genocidal, patriarchal systems that white supremacy created. It took a long time for us to even start to acknowledge that those systems exist, which goes back to that story I was telling about my father in 1980.

We were not talking about suicide when I was a child the way we talk about suicide now. It's taken decades to change our dialogue around mental health. While a lot of people want things to change quickly, sometimes slow and steady wins the race.

I would love for things to be different right now, for hate to be removed from our lexicon, and I also see that the impact I am making on the world today may not be obvious to me in this lifetime.

Not everybody is going to love the conversation, and not everybody is going to agree on it. That is okay. The point is to do our best to lead from our heart and our soul. When we do so, we become less certain and less polarized. We begin to listen and to hear what others are experiencing.

It's important to have conversations without expectations or assumptions. Allow yourself to think of conversations as opportunities to be vulnerable, to surrender, and to listen.

When we engage in this way, we end up living in a space where all things are possible. I can both misunderstand what you are saying and find common ground with you at the same time.

"

Part of being a leader is gracefully leading people down a path of awakening of how ingrained fear and polarization is all throughout society. True rebellion approaches change with love.

"

It pulls us out of this polarizing, 'us versus them' way of thinking, which is what is required to maintain all of these oppressive structures. Capitalism, white supremacy, and misogyny continue to perpetuate if we are unwilling to listen to each other.

Approaching life and leadership from a space of both/and, and entering into the conversation without this rigid, 'this is how it has to be' way of thinking, opens all of us up the possibility of working together to change how we lead and how our communities thrive.

The reason people crave connection is not necessarily to find an answer to their problems. People want to feel seen, heard, and witnessed.

We are grappling with such big concepts globally right now, such as racism, sexism, politics, and global climate change. These are huge problems not just in the United States, but around the world.

We ask, "What are we going to do to staunch the global climate catastrophe?" I think we are asking the wrong question. I believe we need to connect with what is happening at a community level and ask, "What do we need?" What we need here in Oregon to fight forest fires is not the same thing that is needed in Florida to deal with hurricanes.

“

When we love with our whole hearts we engage in a revolutionary action. We make ourselves vulnerable, we open ourselves up to heartbreak and disappointment while at the same time opening ourselves up to feelings of blissed out joy that cause our entire worlds to explode in heavenly expansion.

”

The word 'fight' creates a response in us as if we are somehow in a war or a battle. Perhaps if we started to take that language out of our vocabulary we would realize that there isn't a battle to be fought. Most of the people we connect with in our daily lives at work or in our communities don't want to fight. They want to be heard.

When we start to collect the solutions, the common web among all of them starts to bubble to the surface. We start to think about how we are leaders in our own world and how we come up with solutions not by ourselves, but by connecting with others and asking different questions.

We cannot hold all the answers. It's impossible. We are each only one person.

We are being invited to transform and redefine leadership. Leadership is not necessarily a top-down concept of, 'I'm the expert, you're the people.' That's not the scenario people are asking for.

The Earth works in balance and harmony. If we acknowledge that we are 'humans being', that we are part of the planet because we are naturally occurring beings on the planet, then we can start to think about how to bring things into balance and harmony in terms of the collective.

“

Your soul is craving the freedom to be the entirety of who you are. That is what is ready to emerge right now.

That means we need you to lead from your heart and your intuition. When we are compassionate, kind, and loving towards ourselves, then we are compassionate, kind, and loving towards other people.

When we admit that we don't have all the answers and rise to the occasion of bringing things into harmony, that all-or-nothing, either/or, zero-sum game becomes irrelevant. We work intuitively and recognize that we are working as partners, rather than against each other's ideas.

A lot of leaders, people in positions of power in particular, have decided on the way they want to connect with other people. They don't ask, "How do you want to connect with me?" Instead, they say, "This is how I'm going to connect with you."

If we pull ego out of it and truly connect to heart-centered leadership, then leaders will start to ask, "How can we come together?" What a revolutionary way of thinking. This creates an opening for compassionate, heart-centered leadership that allows us to solve problems in innovative and revolutionary ways.

“

Our ego tells us there can't possibly be enough love to go around and we don't deserve that love. This is a lie.

The reason we avoid leading this way is because of the potential for chaos. If I ask people, "How do you want to connect with me?" and 50 different people on the team have a different answer to the question, that is going to burden me. I'm going to have a lot more work to do.

In reality, there is a common thread among all of the answers you receive when you ask the question, "How do you want to connect with me?" There will be something that bubbles to the surface and says, "Oh, this is the common thread. This is the way the majority of these people want to connect with me."

There are always going to be outliers. That's just data collection. If you ask the same question over and over again and don't feel like you are moving towards what you want or what you envision for the world, then you are asking the wrong question.

“

May the divine help you see your worthiness in the vision for your place in the world. May you be infused with the strength and loving light of God and be held in joy as you do your work in the world.

HOT LASAGNA

Soulful leadership is very traditional, but not necessarily in Western European culture. Soulful leadership requires admitting that you don't have the answer. That is an ancient way of leading.

There is a movie called 'Life over Lithium' about lithium mining in Nevada. It is a 17-minute movie that completely altered my thinking about the climate crisis. It is about Paiute-Shoshone and

Bannock people who have been determined by mining companies to live in 'sacrifice zones' in the land near the mines. This is a story about corporations and governments putting profits over people.

The rationale is built on the notion that electric cars are the best answer to the climate crisis. This allows people to believe that it is okay that some people are going to die because of lithium mining. Companies have determined that they are in the sacrifice zone. Nevermind that these people have lived on this land for thousands of years; we are going to kill them for electric cars. This whole scenario has devastated me.

I don't know the solution to this problem. I do know that illegally setting up a mine without going through the proper channels just so we can make sure the Green New Deal continues in this country isn't the way. I do know that we have to start talking about how human beings are being used as sacrificial lambs to support the mining of lithium.

If we truly care about this planet, and if we say we want a better environment and that electric cars are going to save the world, then we have to look at how destructive lithium mining is. It's not going to save the world.

Lithium mining (any mining, really) is destructive to the soil, birds, animals, plants, people, and all living things in the area of the mine. International mining companies are coming in and mining on United States soil without going through the proper channels. They are not taking into account the environmental impact because it is Native people living in sacrifice zones, and historical rationale has dehumanized Indigenous people so much that we have created a mentality that it is okay to continue destructive practices that allow them to die in the name of progress.

I do not know how we can fix this. I wonder if we are too far gone as a people. I do know that if we are going to address the climate crisis in an intentional way, lithium mining isn't going to help.

I don't have all the answers, but I know in the depths of my soul that the answer is not to kill human beings for a mine.

"

If you feel that tug, that pull, that calling that comes from deep in your belly. Listen. It is the voice that you have been told to ignore and it is the voice that you cannot deny. What is calling to you?

"

In terms of soulful leadership, the question we have to ask here is, “Have we gone so far down the road that it doesn’t matter?”

That’s a hard question to ask. Have we gone so far down the road of the Green New Deal that it doesn’t matter what destructive things we are doing to the planet to earn a profit? Is it okay to place profit margins on the backs of the land, endangered species, and the people?

I believe engaging in soulful leadership means admitting that we have gone too far.

I feel this profound grief coming from the planet. I’m a soulful, intuitive leader, and like you, I am deeply woven with the earth. I wonder if part of what we are all feeling collectively is the knowledge that it’s too far gone. It’s like we are holding onto everything so tightly because we know there may actually be nothing we can do.

That might be the hard truth of it.

Each one of us has a different lens through which we operate. People we consider to be decision-makers, policymakers, CEOs, directors, and leaders operate based on the idea of top-down leadership. They are under the assumption that everyone who works beneath them, or is their client or student, wants the same success that they have.

Many leaders say things like, "I can't imagine why people wouldn't want to buy a home or a car. Why not have a job where you work 30 or 40 hours a week and have insurance? Don't you want to have insurance? Everybody wants insurance!"

They have a very standardized vision of what people want, what family is, what a home is, and what success looks like. They ask things like, "Don't you want to be a billionaire CEO? Don't you want to have all this power and control over people? Don't you want to be a professor? Don't you want to be a researcher? Don't you want to be a teacher? Why would you want to just work at the gas station? Why wouldn't you want more?"

It goes back to this idea of extraction. The American dream is to have more and more and more. That's the concept of globalized capitalism.

We assume people want more when actually they just want to be nurtured and loved. They want to be held. They want to feel heard by the leaders in their community. They want to feel connected to the mystery of the universe.

"

What we feed on sustains us. If you remain hungry for judgment then that is the energy that will feed you. If you remain hungry for joy then joy is your sustenance.

"

People want to feel like they are seen rather than feeling invisible. That's why I always ask homeless people for their names, and they always say, "Oh, you want to know who I am?" I say, "Yeah, I sure do."

When we stop dehumanizing other people and start recognizing our shared humanity, then we will stop assuming what people want and need and realize that what we are all looking for is to be loved and recognized as a person.

That's a very vulnerable thing to say, especially for leaders, CEOs, and people in power. But at the end of the day, that is what we all want.

We want to be nurtured. We want to be happy. We want to be angry and know that is okay, too. We want to feel connected. The desire to feel tender can be seen in the toughest of warriors. The desire to feel rage can be seen in the gentlest of spirits.

All we want is to be held in the beauty of who we are as people.

"

We are all magic. We all have a little ball of light within each one of us that is our guide. It sits right there below our heart glowing with a lovely golden hue. Your power comes from within you. It is placed there divinely by God and the Universe. Go ahead, look within...it might be a faint light but it is there waiting for you to see it.

"

As you absolve yourself of the assumption that everyone needs or wants the same things, we begin to acknowledge people when they say, "I need more office supplies to do my job. I need time off so I can be with my husband who's dying of cancer. I need more work because I don't have enough. We've divided this out to a thousand other people, so I don't have a voice in what I'm doing anymore. I need a different job." When we start asking people what they need, the dialogue we have with them completely changes.

When I taught policy and advocacy classes in schools of Social Work, I would tell this story of a homeless man I knew named Ray.

I loved Ray. He used to sit outside our little post office. He and I would talk every time I went to mail a package. At that time, I was going to the post office almost every day for a month. Ray and I would sit down and chat while he smoked a cigarette.

He had cancer, and you could visibly see it on the top of his head. It was terrible. One day, I said to him, “Ray, what do you need?”

Remember, this is the question I want you to ask. Not, “What do you want? How can I help you?” but, “What do you need?”

Ray looked at me. I thought he was going to say, “A ride to the hospital would be great.” Clearly, in my head, he would be thinking, ‘My cancer is very bad right now.’ I was thinking a thousand different things.

He said, “I just need some hot lasagna.” I said, “Okay, I’ll go get you some hot lasagna. Do you want anything else?” He said, “No, I just really want some hot lasagna. That would be really good right now." I said, "Ray, don't move. You stay right here. Don't move."

I went and got him hot lasagna, a salad, some ice cream, and some bread from a restaurant in town. Of course, he moved while I was gone. I was driving in circles around town looking for Ray. When I saw him, I rolled down my window.

I shouted, "Hey!" He turned around and said, "Dr. Bird!" I said, "I got your food." He started sobbing. "Nobody ever brings the hot lasagna," he said.

When I asked Ray what he needed, I made a thousand different assumptions about what he would say because he had cancer. Here was this homeless man with an open wound on his head who I thought would want me to drive him to the hospital, and all he wanted was hot lasagna. I was making assumptions about what someone else needed based on what I would need if it were me.

“

We are beloved. We are divine. We are sacred.

We have to stop assuming what people need based on what we have. When we help people based on the needs they prioritize, we get an entirely different view of what our communities are and what they can be.

We find commonalities and threads in our experiences when we realize that someone just wants hot lasagna.

That is a very primal desire. "I just want something to comfort me. I just want something that will make me feel good. I want something to make me feel nourished and held. I want comfort food. I want comfort."

If we allow people to have a voice and space for their own experiences, then we find the common threads needed to build a collective community.

That gives us the strength to navigate the unknown and to be comfortable not knowing what's going to happen next with the economy, the planet, elections, or our families and friends. Those threads help us navigate our grief.

"

Every heartache, every struggle, every loss, every fear has led us to this moment of opportunity to make lasting, focused, rebellious change. We cannot fail if we follow the whispers of the heart.

"

You can change your entire life and your community by listening to what the people around you need.

What if productivity wasn't the end game? I invite us to shift the narrative away from productivity and towards being okay with not having all of the answers.

The aim of soulful leadership is to help people be more accepting of their feelings and the feelings of others. That does not necessarily mean people will be happier. The end game is completely disrupting the way we have been doing things up to this point. We must recognize that the way we connect with people, lead people, and assume what people need and want isn't working anymore.

It's destroyed our planet, our sense of collective community, and the fabric of who we are as intricately woven human beings.

We continue relying on human, earth-bound, and ocean-bound resources to the point of decimation. We are destroying people's souls and minds by making them work too much. We are leading them to think that they don't have good ideas, they are not smart enough, and they have to go get another degree in order to have an impact on their communities. There is a limit to what we can do.

"

What would happen if we admitted that we are sad about what is happening in the world and we took little tiny steps each day to shift the tide in our own backyard? I think we would come together as a collective force. I think we would shed what doesn't serve our higher mission. I think we would stop shaming and blaming each other for our choices. I think we would give ourselves lots of oxygen and breathe.

"

The more unsure we are about the future, the more we are inclined to grip tighter onto what we know. Soulful leadership is an invitation for us to open up and allow ourselves to dig into a creative, curious process and wonder about what we cannot see.

Leading from the heart requires that we be willing to step into spaces where we don't have all the answers, where it's uncertain what will happen next, and where we can't see clearly. It's about knowing that we are on the path forward, no matter what.

When we open ourselves up to soulful leadership and start asking people, "What are your ideas? What do you think we could do here? What opportunities do you see for growth? How can we make use of our collective ideas if we operate from a space of potential?" then everything becomes limitless.

As long as we are living, we are still moving forward. This means that each day we are afforded the opportunity to walk into the unknown, venture into the darkness, knowing that eventually there will be wisdom and light without needing to know how they will manifest.

"

You have plenty of treasures in all areas of your life. You have enough brain power, you have enough innovation, you have enough guts. Your ideas are exactly what we have been waiting for.

"

You must be willing to go into leadership open-handed instead of close-fisted. When we acknowledge that we do not know everything as people, we are invited into a collective community. You become a leader not so you can tell people what the answer is, but to collectively ask what the best answer is.

If we are willing to navigate the unknown, we open the capacity to genuinely engage with the people in front of us. When we're willing to be uncertain, not know what comes next, and accept that we don't have all the answers, we'll be less punitive. We can allow ourselves to exist in a space of curiosity. We don't have to tell people how to do things.

When we stop trying to predict outcomes and give each other grace for missteps and learning, then we are given the space to allow the divine in to do the work. This type of leadership then allows us to open ourselves to endless possibilities instead of demanding answers from our colleagues and communities.

The act of engaging in soulful leadership is an act of Graceful Revolution. The world is changing rapidly. This chapter is an invitation to trust and have faith. When we honor the divine in ourselves, people in power and in leadership positions can learn a different way of thinking. My vision for the world is one where people like myself have a voice that is honored, respected, and heard. I want to disrupt the narrative that controlling other people is the only way to lead.

“

Dear one, I give you permission at this time to be whatever it is you need to be. Remember to listen to that inner guide inside you. There is a little voice in there. Sometimes it is quietly whispering, sometimes it is pounding down the door, but it is always there telling you exactly what you need to hear. Listen to the whispers of your heart. They are your guiding light.

”

When leaders recognize our shared humanity, they begin to understand that what we do to one person, we do to all people.

There is another way to lead. A way that takes us out of either/or thinking and invites us into the mystery of the both/and. In acknowledging our shared humanity, we disrupt systemic oppression and begin to run companies, governments, and organizations in a way that honors people and the planet.

I want to reach impactful people, such as CEOs, politicians, or any officials who have the ability to make a deep impact on the world but have not yet found their own inner morals and ethical voices because they have been distorted by capitalistic authority. These leaders know there is a better way, and they are ready to do the work to change.

This is your invitation to ask a different question. Instead of asking, “How can I help?” we must start asking, “What do you need?” When we ask people what they need, our assumptions fade away, because we get a direct response from our community.

I have a prayer on my wall, and part of it talks about going into the darkness and putting your faith into something bigger than you, and how that is safer than following the light along a known way.

We don’t have to know exactly where we are going. We just have to be willing to take the first step on our way.

“

YOU are intricately connected to the vastness of the universe. You are the beauty of the stars.

DISCLAIMER

ABOUT THE AUTHOR

Dr. Melissa Bird is a descendant of the Shivwits Band of Paiutes. She is an internationally recognized lay preacher, author, healer, and podcaster. Dr. Bird has spent nearly three decades teaching workshops on spiritual and social justice and revolution. When she's not working, Melissa can be found reading while drinking Earl Grey tea with heavy cream. She lives in Corvallis, Oregon, with her husband, three children, and two dogs.

www.ingramcontent.com/pod-product-compliance
Lightning Source LLC
LaVergne TN
LVHW052338100826
845147LV00020B/1103
* 9 7 8 1 6 1 3 4 3 1 8 7 0 *